Faces

Faces

A Collection of Stories and Poems
by
M. G. Pasha

Life Rattle Press
Toronto, Canada

Faces
Copyright © 2018 by Manahil Ghina Pasha

All rights reserved. The use of any part of this publication reproduced or transmitted in any form or by any means, electronic, mechanical, photocopying, recording or otherwise, or stored in a retrieval system without the prior consent of the author is an infringement of the copyright law.

Life Rattle New Publishers Series
ISSN 978-1-897161-84-5
ISBN 978-1-987936-65-0

Published by Life Rattle Press
Toronto, Canada

Typeset and Cover Design by Manahil Pasha
Cover Rendering by Maryam Pasha
Copyedited by Nick West

To my family. Our experiences are more than just memories. They are stories: vessels that carry our essence.

Table of Contents

Faces	11
Peach Paint	15
Mrs. Meyers	23
Dragged	31
Dissent	43
The Angry Cheeto	53
The Biannual Carrom Tournament	65
Ghost Stories	75
Grandiose Gestures	91

Faces

Your kindness is in your smile.
Its curving, light lines
form under your cheeks and
lead to your gleaming, ragged teeth
that burst out in a happy guffaw.

Your anger is in your tongue.
It whips out in cold fury,
pulling your lips up on one side
and forming a harsh crack
down your forehead.

Your sadness is in your eyes.
Glazed over with unshed tears,
your lower lip trembles,
and your eyebrows pull upwards
in silent plea.

To me you are not your face,
but your faces.

I

I often wonder how you perfected your sneer
at such a young age;
Your curled lip and flared nostrils,
and the glint of wicked glee in your eyes.

Did someone teach you,
or did it come to you like breathing?

Peach Paint

I hate Michael. He's in my first-grade class. Michael's the type of kid whose face is stuck in a perpetual sneer. His nostrils flare, and his eyes stretch, and I hate him. I hate him because he has a loud, obnoxious voice that demands to be heard. When he speaks, his nasal-whine drowns out my own thoughts, and blurs the words of the book I'm reading.

"Reading again? You nerd," he says, and I'm ripped out of *The Green School Mystery*. I blink up at him and scowl, then look back at my book, and scowl again. I've forgotten which character I suspected of being the nickel thief.

During P.E. on the grasshopper-filled field behind the school, I stand inside the goalpost because nobody else wants to be goalie. Michael is on my team playing offense. He runs towards the ball, but the other kid gets past him. I move too slow. The ball rolls past me into the goal. Michael runs over, red-faced and sweaty, to yell at me.

"How could you let the ball in? You're such a loser," he hisses. I cringe. My head begins to pound under the hot sun. I turn around and walk towards Miss Hanes. My team is already busy trying to score the next goal.

"Miss Hanes, I don't feel so good. I don't think I can play anymore." I blink up at Miss Hanes, with my hand on my head. She smiles down at me, her red hair shining in the sunlight.

"That's alright, Mina. Why don't you go and rest on the bleachers?"

༄

It's break time. We've gone through our spelling, and I've done my readings, and coloured in my map, and matched the words on my worksheet.

Now I finally get some time to play on the computer. I measure the distance from my desk to the computer with my eye. It sits on a table across the room; a clunky grey box that holds bright, colourful characters. I know I can only make my date with the purple octopus in JumpStart if I get there first, but Michael's chair is closer to the monitor. Michael catches me staring. A slow, feral grin creeps across his face—worse than any sneer. He jumps from his seat, strides to the monitor, and gets there first.

Michael always gets there first.

༄

Michael comes to school every day with Fruit Roll Ups or Rice Krispies, or even some coveted Lunchables. He hands out little pieces of cheese and crackers to a few simpering classmates. I take a bite of my browning apple slices.

༄

Art time comes around, and I don't care about Michael anymore. It's just me and the paper and the pretty colours, and I'm determined to draw the coolest 3D house, just like Father showed me. I spend the hour erasing and redrawing the lines, fitting the roof just right and making sure my family's smiling faces are visible through the window. I can't wait to show Miss Hanes.

"Look here, everyone! Hasn't Michael drawn the most wonderful house?" We all look where Miss Hanes is pointing. Michael's house has two floors and a balcony. I don't show Miss Hanes my drawing.

ఌ

Next art time, Miss Hanes tells us we're going to paint self-portraits. At least we won't be drawing houses, I think to myself.

"Alright everyone! Line up so I can give you your paint," Miss Hanes says. "Just tell me which colours you would like, and I'll pour them onto your plates." Chairs scrape across the linoleum floor as everyone rushes eagerly towards Miss Hanes.

Michael tries to push his way in front of me in line, but I block him.

"I was here first." I frown at him. He gives me a sheepish grin and steps back.

When it's my turn, I glance down at my pink t-shirt and blue jeans and hold up my plate for Miss Hanes.

"I think I'm going to have to mix some white and red for my t-shirt, Miss Hanes."

"That's right Mina! And some black for your hair and some—" She pauses and frowns at the peach paint she's squeezed onto my plate and holds it up to my arm.

"Well that doesn't seem to match." She examines the other colours and then mixes some black paint into the peach.

"There you go Mina. That matches much better." I stare at the muddy, marbled mess on my plate. It doesn't match my skin.

I glance back at Michael while I trudge back to my desk. He smirks at me as Miss Hanes pours some peach paint to match his face.

I hate Michael.

II

You've got little crinkles of kindness
around your green eyes,
and a round, rosy complexion.
Your grin spreads and grows
and sows hope in the beholder.

Does your barbed tongue
envy the face that drips
poisonous lies better
than it ever could?

Mrs. Meyers

I tiptoe down the stairs. I should be sleeping. It's past my bedtime and I have to wake up early for my third-grade spelling test in the morning, but my parents' hushed, inquisitive voices have woken me. I pause on the third step down as my sister's guttural sobs seep into my sleep-riddled mind. My stomach growls. I want some milk. For a moment I debate interrupting the scene unfolding below, but curiosity wins out and I crouch onto the step to listen in.

"I don't want to go to school tomorrow! I hate grade four!" Mahira wails.

"Just tell us what's wrong! Did someone say

something to you?" I can sense the simmering annoyance in Father's voice.

"No-o." Mahira's response is punctuated by a loud hiccup.

"Look, I am getting angry now." Mother's stern voice floats up to my huddled figure. "Maybe we should speak to your teacher tomorrow about how our daughter is crying at home about school, hmm?"

"Nooo d-don't do that!" I can imagine Mahira's face, eyes wide with the fear of inevitable humiliation.

"Then tell me," Mother demands. Mahira's sobs ebb as she finally yields, speaking with a trembling voice broken by sharp gasps.

"It's Mrs. Meyers. She y-yelled at me today. She called me st-stupid. She's so mean to me."

"What?" Father says in his gruff voice, "Why would she do that?"

"She said I didn't know multiplication. The other kids learned it last year, but I didn't. She made fun of me in front of everyone!"

Father sighs. We moved from Windsor to Houston before the school year started and were behind on some of the curriculum.

"It's okay," he says. "Don't worry about it. We'll just practice at home and catch you up. Then your teacher won't yell at you okay?" Mahira quiets and stops sniffling.

"Okay," she mutters, unsure.

Yeah right, I think. Teachers can't be that bad. Mahira never liked school anyway. I really want some milk.

☙

The next year, I'm in fourth grade. I sit next to my new best friend, Helen, listening to Mrs. Meyers explain how to do a "mad minute" quiz.

"Skip the questions you don't kno— Ewwwww!" The sudden change of tone makes me jump. Mrs. Meyers looks towards me.

"Ewww, that is disgusting!" She exclaims again, louder and more aggravated than before. She lifts her hand and points a single crooked finger towards me. I freeze.

"Do you see that everyone?" She asks, twisting her face into a nauseated expression. "Look! Helen is picking at a huuuuuge scab on her knee!"

I glance to my left, letting out a breath. Helen's knuckles turn white as she nervously clutches at her pencil. I see a blush creep up her neck, working its way through the olive tone of her skin. I stiffen.

"Ew Helen, that is so gross! Isn't Helen so gross everyone? Ewwwwwwwwwwwwww"

Mrs. Meyers draws out the word, building up volume and hitting a crescendo, leaving it lingering in the air. I gape at her. Her hands are placed firmly on her hips, her mouth is twisted into a sneer, and her eyebrows are bunched up so tight, they touch in the middle of her forehead. A chorus of "ew's" echo from around the room. The boys snicker. Mrs. Meyers glares at Helen who avoids her eyes, looking down to her lap. Her ears burn a dull scarlet, and her eyes shine, holding back tears. She threads her fingers together and places her hands onto the desk.

"That is just disgusting Helen. Who picks at a

scab? Ew. Okay? Don't do that in my classroom. Next time I catch you, you're staying in for recess. Nobody wants to see that." Mrs. Meyers sneers one last time, and then refocuses on her paper.

"Now, where was I? Oh right, the mad minutes!" She continues her explanation, ignoring the boys who still snicker behind their hands.

I peek at Helen again. Her eyes don't move from the worksheet in front of her. Her shoulders are bunched together, the collar of her uniform polo squishing behind her neck.

"Alright then class, you have one minute to complete the entire sheet of questions. Aaaand, go!"

I start writing. Beside me, Helen raises a shaking hand—her grip tight—and starts scraping answers onto her worksheet.

III

Long deep lines.
They bend around from your nose
down to the edges of your mouth.

Short, cracked lines.
They branch out from
the corners of your eyes.

Like the roots of a tree,
and its rings,
your lines speak a language
of their own.

Dragged

We receive the summons late on a Friday afternoon. Father arrives home from *Jumma* (Friday prayers) and announces that Munir Sadiq Sahib, the Nasir Academy principal, requests that my sister and I come to the mosque to teach at the Sunday school.

Teach at Sunday school? What does that even mean? When I was younger, we didn't have a Sunday school. The adults would just herd us children into some unused corner of the mosque and sic an old auntie on us. It was boring. We repeated Arabic prayers over and over again until we knew them by heart, and when the adults were finally finished their important meetings, we were collected by our mothers and taken home; reciting the words the whole way. Up until high school, I knew plenty of prayers in Arabic, but had no idea what they meant; it was an incomplete education.

So, what am I supposed to teach? I'm not some old uncle, stuffed with years of wisdom and tales of faith-inducing incidents. My knowledge of Islam is fragmented and insufficient and basic. I know the five pillars of Islam and the articles of faith and I've got some sections of the Qur'an memorised, but that's it.

I mean, I guess I know how to teach in theory—having taken a single university credit in teaching—and I know how children work in general, considering how many children surround me at family gatherings (14 and counting). And I mean, I used to be a child once, right? But I was quiet and shy, and lonely: the opposite of a group of kids. How can I possibly handle a classroom of wild, whiny children?

But I can't say no! Everyone knows everyone in

the Jama'at (community), and how disrespectful would it be to deny the request of an elder? I'd have to don a niqab to hide the shame! To be requested by name—well, "Haaris's sister" suffices as a name in this case, I guess—and then refuse? Blasphemy!

☙

The following Sunday, I drag myself out of bed, skip breakfast, and arrive to Uncle Munir's office at 10:45 AM sharp with Father and my sister.

Father introduces us, and after a quiet *Salam*, I take a seat in one of the mismatched maroon chairs that seem to be placed haphazardly around the office. Across from me is Uncle Munir's large wrap-around cherry-wood desk, a colony of printing mistakes, paperclips, and used staples. The office itself isn't very large, so when another two ladies join us, it feels more like a closet. Uncle Munir introduces them as Auntie Naila, a Sunday school veteran and advisor, and Mariam, a new administrative recruit. My sister, Father and I sit in a row, and Auntie Naila and Mariam stand behind us, out of view.

"Thank you for coming in!" Uncle Munir starts off with a large grin, settling himself down in his own chair, fingers splayed across the desk in front of him. I watch his chin waggle as he speaks. His trim, greying beard crawls up the sides of his face and disappears seamlessly into the grey, woolly, Persian hat perched on his head.

"We really need some fresh blood to come in and teach here at Nasir Academy, and so I'm grateful to you for volunteering so readily." I squeeze my lips together to avoid grimacing, or else presenting anything but the most respectful of expressions.

After the customary small talk to garner our educational backgrounds, Uncle Munir's expression turns more serious, and he leans forward, gaze squarely on us, as if to impart some great secret.

"You know, we really need some younger teachers here. In the past we've had some…what you would call, 'aunties', and it hasn't really worked out." He raises his hands and draws quotation marks in the air. "We've gotten a lot of complaints from parents and teachers and, you know, children don't want to come to school anymore. So, I sat in some of the classes to monitor the teaching, and I wasn't happy with what I saw…" His face droops in disappointment as he releases a tired sigh.

I glance to my right, and my sister raises her eyebrows in response. My mind wanders to our own childhood teachers: wrinkled, old ladies who glared at us with dark, kohl-slathered eyes if we produced any sound they hadn't sanctioned. Don't speak. That was the big rule. And if the auntie was speaking an incomprehensible mix of Urdu and Punjabi, well, just listen.

Uncle Munir raises his elbows to rest on the desk and steeples his fingers, eyes far away as he continues. "Well, suffice to say, they were too strict for my taste, and they scolded the children too much, and…well I didn't like it." His roaming, disappointed eyes meet mine for a second, before moving on. "I believe that the children should learn through rewards instead of punishment. This should be a fun Sunday school."

I nod along to his earnest, impromptu speech, and his lips quirk upwards slightly. If Uncle Munir had been my teacher when I was a kid, maybe 'fun Sunday school' wouldn't be an oxymoron.

"I'm hoping that by bringing in some more teachers from the younger, Canadian generation, you can mesh well with the kids, and understand them better. Right?" He purses his lip and blinks at me, waiting for a response. I arrange my face into a focused look and nod again, before squeaking out a reply.

"Yes, of course!" I peek at my sister who is playing with a piece of lint on her dress. I wish I had sat in her seat instead of where I am, directly in Uncle Munir's line of vision.

"Good," Uncle Munir says, and then reaches to his left for a pile of four brightly coloured books. He slides out a bright green book with the words "Level 2 Syllabus" emblazoned in red on the cover and holds it out towards me. I stare at the book, bewildered.

"We have a syllabus?" I take it from his hand, flip through it quickly, then pass it onto my sister.

"Yes." Uncle Munir chuckles. "We've been running the school for over a decade now. A couple of years ago, we had around 300 students, and dedicated teachers, but over time, a lot of the staff left and students stopped coming. It's my fault too." His shoulders sag as these words leave his mouth, and I have the strange urge to deny them. "I couldn't spend as much time and effort as I should have with my various responsibilities, and the school started declining." His voice fades into a forlorn sigh.

I stay quiet and trade a look with my sister, who shrugs at me. There is another beat of silence. Then, with renewed animation, Uncle Munir leans back in his bulky office chair, breaking into a warm smile. His eyes crinkle slightly to reveal the soft indents around them.

"Maybe with more volunteers like you, we can bring this school back to where it was before, hmm?" I give a quick nod, and a 'yeah' of affirmation, perking up with hope.

Maybe I could do this and avoid the shame of denying an elder's request, I think to myself. He isn't looking for an auntie! I don't need to be old or wrinkly or wise. Even if I don't feel ready for it, I can make do. They're just kids, not monsters. Uncle Munir's smile widens, and he adopts a commanding tone, straightening into business mode.

"Good, so I was thinking you two can be assistants for a little while, and circle around helping other teachers or co-teach a class when the need arises. That will work for this semester. Then next semester, if everything goes well, I'm hoping you can take over our level two classes, one for the girls and one for the boys. You can decide who you want to teach later. Does that sound good?" We nod our assent, and Uncle Munir claps his hands together once to signal the end of the discussion and then turns to speak to Auntie Naila. My sister leans towards me.

"I call the girls," she whispers. "You can deal

with the boys. Hah! Good luck." And just like that, it's decided.

"Baji Naila," Uncle Munir brings our attention back to him. "If you could take these girls and introduce them to the other teachers and give them a bit of an orientation, that would be great."

Auntie Naila nods and ushers us out the door as Uncle Munir lingers in his office to catch up with Father. His patient voice peters out as we move down the hall into the main area of the mosque. I hear the sounds of dramatic squeals and children's thumping feet.

"Are they always this loud?" I ask. Auntie Naila gives me a pitying nod.

"Well, they're on their break right now, which is why they're running, but generally, yes. They can be quite loud," she explains. I take in what Auntie Naila says. I hang my head and gulp. My heart pounds as we get close to the children.

IV

I should have known
from the glazed eyes
down to the slack-jaw,
that my words were falling
on deaf ears.

After all, it was your
squinty eyes,
and guilty glance,
that heard the crash
more than your ears.

Dissent

The grey-carpeted room in the center of the mosque's office area is known as the "old library." Dozens of metal chairs line the stretch of empty white walls that are scuffed from years of abuse. Two old couches are stuffed in a corner at the head of the room and a custom, beech wood podium stands next to them. If this little hall had once been lined with full bookshelves, I cannot imagine it. Now, it is a sparse, multipurpose space: a storage room, a classroom, a shortcut through the mosque, and an occasional meeting space. A few unfortunate members of the community know it by its most used function: the viewing room.

The children who attend Nasir Academy are unaware of this particular function, of course. For today, it is their classroom. They might be a bit disturbed to know that behind one of the doors leading out of the hall, sits a stack of plain, wood coffins. Or worse. They might be too interested.

Trying to configure the room into a classroom, I order the children—there are eight of them today—to set up some chairs in a semicircle. I eye a wobbly plastic table. It looks like it might collapse if I move it away from the wall. I sigh. In lieu of a teacher's desk, I might have to keep my binders in my lap today.

The first hour goes well: we recite a prayer for the well-being of our parents, and then move on to a short reading on the life of the Prophet Muhammad$^{(SAW)}$. The boys like reading aloud, even if they are terrible at it. It soon becomes a chore to listen to their stunted pronunciations.

In the second hour, there is dissent.

"*Mina Baji* (meaning older sister), when are we getting our snack?" I squint at Eqaan, a thick-haired boy, and stifle a groan. It's always the fidgety ones. This one hasn't stopped pulling the strings of his backpack since he's sat down.

"I'm not sure. We'll have to wait for Auntie to bring the snacks to us. Let's just wait a little bit longer." With that we return to reading, but we only get through one paragraph.

"But I'm hungry!" Eqaan whines.

I clench my jaw and look around. Oh no. Eight expectant eyes staring straight at me, and not the book they should be reading. I glance at the time, and frown. It's 12:45. Odd, it's 15 minutes past when we usually start our snack break.

"Alright, let's take our break right now," I say, "I'll just go down the hall real quick and check on the snack situation, okay?"

"Umm, can we play a game?" Asks Ayaan. I narrow my eyes at the short, buck-toothed boy.

"Which game?" I ask. Taking my question as acceptance, the boys start shouting out their answers.

"Tag!"

"Freeze tag!"

"Hide and seek!"

"No way." I keep my voice firm. I stand up, towering over them. "This is not a playground. We're still inside a mosque. So that means nothing that involves running around or poking people."

"But there's no running in hide and seek!" Whines Ayaan.

"There's nowhere to hide in this room, and I don't want you guys touching anything, okay? This is a mosque, not the park." After receiving a chorus of disappointed "okays," I nod. I move to leave, calling out behind me.

"Why don't you all play some Heads Up, Seven Up? I'll be back in two minutes. Don't burn this place down!"

It takes a bit longer than two minutes. I meet Auntie Naila in the entrance hall as she sets up cupcakes for the bake sale. She's an intimidating, older lady, in charge of snacks among other administrative duties.

"Assalamu alaikum Auntie. I'm sorry, but I didn't get the snacks for my class today," I say awkwardly. My hands try to find purchase in the non-existent pockets of my coat, before falling back to my sides.

"Oh, sorry dear," she says, pausing to look at me. "Well did you hand in your attendance?" She stares up at me over the rims of her glasses.

"Um…" Under my hijab, heat creeps up my neck. "No, I didn't."

"Well there you go. That's how we determine how many students need a snack. For now, just tell me how many students you have today, and I'll send someone with the snacks." She pulls out a pen and a pad of yellow sticky notes from her pocket.

"Um, including me there's nine of us today," I say.

"Alright dear," Auntie Naila says, writing down the number on her sticky notes. "You go on ahead and I'll send them to you soon."

"Okay Auntie, Thank you!"

The situation resolved, I head back to the old library. A sudden yell echoes into the hallway and makes me quicken my pace. As I step through the door, I see Ayaan cowering behind the podium at the front of the room. The other seven boys are scattered around. A few are calling out Ayaan's name. Hide and seek. I told them not to play hide and seek!

"What is going on in here?" I thunder, throwing Ayaan what I hope is a daunting glare. His panicked eyes turn to me.

In his haste to stand up, Ayaan wedges himself between the podium and the wall, driving into it. It teeters forward, almost tipping over. Ayaan pauses, still stuck in a half-crouch behind it.

"Careful!" I hiss, my eyes widening.

Too late. Ayaan stands up. I watch—as if in slow motion—as his shoulder bumps into the flat top of the podium. It tips. The podium crashes to the ground, narrowly missing another boy standing in front of it. Sharp gasps and a screeched "Oh my God!" fill the room. In a blink, I race over to help Ayaan, who has fallen over with the podium.

"Are you okay?" I look him over and he nods. I turn towards the other students in the room who are frozen, standing against the back wall.

"What were you thinking? I told you not to play hide and seek or touch anything in this room!" Ayaan looks down nervously. The other boys stand shame-faced. "Break is over. You will eat your snacks in your chairs. Now go and sit down!" My voice has risen to a shriek, still a bit shell-shocked. The boys stumble back to their seats, heads hanging.

I turn back to haul up the podium myself, grunting with effort, until Ayaan moves to help me. As we put it upright, I hear a crack. My eyes swivel to the front of the podium and widen in horror. There, laying on the ground, is its custom engraved front panel, in three pieces .

"Oooooooh, you're in so much trouble Ayaan!" One of the boys says from behind us. I pick up the three pieces of the panel as Ayaan stands next to me. We are both pale and quiet. And we're both in trouble.

V

Your face transforms
when you recall another.

As though the mere memory
of spittle flying from hateful, puckered lips
and tanned hide-like skin,
forms a mask and solidifies
on your own confused face,
twisting innocence into terror
and moulding revulsion.

The Angry Cheeto

I work my way down the attendance sheet, methodically placing a small "P" in the squares. One for each loud, gossiping boy in the classroom. I glance up to see if "Shayan Qureshi" is here. The mousy 8-year-old sits in the first row wearing a hesitant grin as he listens to a larger boy beside him tell a story. I mark another "P" in the last square and put the attendance down onto the desk nestled in the corner of the classroom.

Aside from me, sitting in front of the white board, there are ten little boys sitting scattered amongst the four rows of wooden, wobbly school desks.

"Alright everyone! Could we please move up to the front? There is plenty of space here in the first rows." My words are met with still, blank faces and I realize I should not have posed a question. I release a long-suffering sigh.

"Everyone in the back two rows, move up to the front. Now." Low voice, hard tone, not too much of a growl, and an unimpressed stare; a hint of disdain without malice. It feels odd to push the rough voice out of my throat, but it works.

There are several groans, before four 10-year olds with drooping shoulders pick up their binders and their bags, and shuffle down the aisle in the middle of the classroom to fight over the seats in the second row. Zain loses. With a pout, he moves up to sit in the front row aisle seat. After a few more seconds of fussing at their desks, the boys finally settle down.

I uncross my arms and push my large round glasses up my nose, coming out of the "I'm waiting" position. I stand up to address my students. They adopt the dopey, loose-jawed expressions that

I attribute to listening.

"Good morning everyone, I thought we could start off today by talking about how your week went!" My overly-cheerful tone makes me cringe. Dial it down, or they won't take you seriously.

Faaz and Mowahid groan loudly at my words. Ibrahim and Aman follow their lead and scrunch up their faces. I send the latter a quick glare that shuts them up. They're still new, still intimidated. In a practiced move, I raise a single dark, withering eyebrow at Faaz and Mowahid.

"Is there a problem, or are you volunteering to go first?" I ask slowly, and hope my tone is scathing enough.

"Can't we talk about dinosaurs and aliens like we did last time? I don't wanna talk about my week. It was boooring." Faaz's high-pitched whining distracts me from his words. I consider his complaint anyway, humming in thought, and survey the hopeful eyes of the other boys. Then, I plop down onto my black rolling chair and throw up my arms in a great show of acquiescence: fond and grudgingly indulgent. The illusion of their victory is important.

"Alright, what does everyone want to talk about, then? I can be nice. Choose anything."

"Aliens!" Faaz exclaims and looks towards the other boys for support.

"We already talked about them last week," I say. "So, we can't talk about them today. And no dinosaurs either!"

"What about Harambe?" Blurts out Zain.

"Donald Trump!" Aman shouts over him

"Spongebob Squarepants!" Yells someone from the second row. I can no longer keep up with the suggestions until Rayan speaks up.

"Yeah, Trump!" He says, and the boys quiet down. In an act of collective agreement, they turn their eager eyes to me; the subject clearly decided. My repertoire of practiced, teacher-esque reactions comes up empty. I blink.

"Um, What about him?" I ask, unsure I'll be able to answer their questions.

"Did you hear him talking about building a

wall?" Rayan asks and a clamour of voices rise up in reply, overlapping and blending into each other.

"Can you believe how racist he is? He said that all Mexicans were criminals!" Aman exclaims, bringing his hands up in front of him in a gesture of disbelief.

"Pfft, I know," Mowahid joins in, looking unimpressed. "And did you hear him bragging about how much money he has?"

"Yeah, he's such a hater. He said he wants to ban all Muslims!" Aman shouts again, crossing his arms in front of him. "I'm so glad I don't live in America!"

"Did you see the crazy memes of him online? He looks like an angry Cheeto!" Giggles Shayan from off to the side, catching Ibrahim's attention.

"A Cheeto? Really?"

"Harambe for president!" Zain yells out again. Like me, he doesn't seem to be following the conversation.

"Ooh did you see the one where his wig flies off? That one was good."

"Ok woah, woah, woah!" I hold my palms up. "Slow down guys. I can't keep up. Raise your hands if you want to say something." There is an impatient pause before ten hands shoot into the air. "Okay, umm…Mowahid."

"My parents don't like him."

"Yeah! Mine too!"

"SAME!"

"Okay, GUYS. Seriously." I'm met with another beat of wide-eyed silence. "How about I ask you what you think? Aman? Do you have something to say?"

"Yeah, umm. Trump is running for president, but he's so racist! Can he actually kick all Muslims and Mexicans out of the country?"

"And why does he hate us so much?" Mowahid looks confused, his face resting in his palm.

"Yeah, not all Muslims are bad! It's not fair!" Rayan cries, pounding his fist on his desk.

"Will he really become president?" Quiet Rohan pipes up, and silence engulfs us once more. I let out a deep breath.

"Okay. I understand what you guys are saying, but I can't respond to anything if you won't let me say a word." Ten bodies squirm with guilt. Aman waits for my reply, his bulbous eyes magnified by glasses.

"To answer your question Aman, I don't think that Trump could just do whatever he wants even if he did become president because, Rohan, in the U.S. constitution—does everyone know what the constitution is?" I am surprised to see nods. "Okay. Well, in the constitution, it says that all Americans have the right to practice whatever religion they want, so kicking anyone out of the country based on their religion is against the law."

"Yeah, but what if he changes the law? The president can do that right?" Rayan's question is unsure, so I figure my answer should be the opposite.

"Rayan, the court system works separate from the president. They would stop him. Probably."

"Yeah, but what if he ignores them, or fires them?" Aman asks, eyes wide and agitated. "He's going to be the president, he can do whatever he wants!"

"Okay, calm down Aman." This time, the derision in my voice is unfeigned. "There's no guarantee that he will become president. Besides, a lot of people like Hilary way more. We're just going to have to trust the Americans. I mean they chose Obama, didn't they?"

Ten heads nod mechanically.

"And he's been a great president, so I don't think there's anything you need to worry about." The boys' expressions range from pensive to skeptical. Mowahid speaks up.

"Hey at least, Justin Trudeau likes us!" A chorus of agreement follows this assertion and I can't help but grin. Ibrahim stands up, palms flat on his desk, and declares:

"I am so glad I'm Canadian!"

VI

Mouths open and close.
Open and close and turn,

With growling words,
and cheery words,
with yelps and whistles and laughter,

That keep our eyes as thin slits,
because we pull our cheeks so high.

The Biannual Carrom Tournament

Eid creeps closer, bringing with it the stress of planning the biannual family get-together. Father is an extension of the couch, still wearing his brown, suede jacket from work. His lunchbox is abandoned at his feet.

"What are we doing this Eid, Father? Have you talked to anybody yet?" I wait as he stares at his phone a little longer before finally placing it down and sighing. He hates this stuff too.

"I don't know. I called everyone but there aren't any plans yet. You're Uncle Mansoor doesn't want to host this time. Says your aunt is too busy taking care of the baby to host." I roll my eyes.

It goes on like this. Uncle Waseem wants to avoid another explosive argument with Mother. Aunt Tayyiba hosted everyone last time and refuses to do it again. Uncle Nasim doesn't want to overwhelm his in-laws, and nobody wants to pay for catering. They want the party, but not the responsibility.

"Okay," I say. "But that only leaves us, and we can't have everyone here, what with Mother's health and all. Can't we just go to a restaurant or something instead?" Father snorts in response.

"What, all thirty-forty of us?" He asks.

"No, just us five, just our family."

"Of course not." Father dismisses my question with a wave of his hand.

"But why? I mean the important part is going to the mosque and praying. We don't have to do a huge party afterwards. People go out to eat all the time!"

"Not people with relatives nearby," he explains in a patronizing tone. "We should be grateful that there are so many of us who can meet and celebrate such a blessed day. Think about my parents. I haven't been able to spend Eid with them in 25 years. We can only skype every year." I don't have a response to that, but I pout anyway, changing the issue.

"I know that, but it's a disaster every year!" Father frowns.

"Oh, stop it Mina. It'll be a chance for you to enjoy some time with everyone."

"Enjoy? Who can enjoy their antics? I can tell you exactly how Eid is gonna go right now, and it definitely won't be fun." Father smirks at me.

"Okay fine." He puts down his phone. "Go ahead. Tell me exactly what's going to happen." I frown at his mocking tone before beginning my tirade.

"The same routine we have every Eid! All the aunties will immediately comment on each other's jewelry and clothing and how much it all cost, even before we step through the door. 'Oh, you got that for 120 dollars. I saw the same suit at the Eid bazaar for 70.'

"And then they'll turn to us kids and comment on our weight or something, like 'Oh Mina, did you gain some weight? You should take care of yourself. Think about your *future*.'

"Then of course, the Uncles' biannual carrom tournament begins, which means nobody is moving for at least an hour. They'll sit there, distracting each other from taking the right shots. They'll talk about 'cut' shots and who gets to drop the queen into the hole. Meanwhile the carrom men (puck-like game pieces) are flying all over the place.

"Aunt Tayyiba in the meantime, is going to get angry at someone because they'll inevitably say something rude to her. She'll scream for a while before she grabs her family and drags them home.

"And then, someone will go, 'Nobody made tea yet? And bring on the dessert!' or 'Wow Sana, did you make that trifle yourself? You're becoming handy in the kitchen!' Which we all know actually means, 'wow it's time we find you a husband.' And then they'll start comparing the girls' cooking skills.

"Obviously we cousins are going to have to run upstairs and have rebellious conversations about how we should go bowling instead because the elders are so dull. And eventually Uncle Nasim and Mansoor will have to go because their babies are crying so much, and that'll be the end of the night!"

I gasp, out of breath. Father's eyes shine with amusement.

"I dare you to say that all in front of them on Eid," he says.

I scoff. Yeah right, I think to myself. I don't have a death wish.

༄

A couple of days later, we arrive at Uncle Nasim's house and Auntie Serosh comes to greet us. She hones in on Mother's ears as soon as we step through the door.

"Salam! Wow, are those earrings new?" She asks, excited, reaching out to touch the earrings. From behind her, Uncle Nasim appears, greeting my dad.

"*Assalamo alaikum.* You're finally here! We've

been waiting for you. Come inside." Uncle Nasim leads father into the living room while we follow. Auntie Tayyiba sits on the nearby dining table, chatting away with my other aunts and comparing notes on their new Eid suits. A square wooden carrom board, with its four corner pockets and flat game pieces is already set up on a small, round table. Uncle Waseem and Uncle Mansoor are seated on either side of the board. They spot Father.

"Oho!" Uncle Mansoor exclaims. "My carrom partner is finally here. Come sit down so we can pocket the queen and beat these two," he says, pointing at my other uncles. I give Father a pointed look; it would be rude to say 'I told you so'. He shrugs and sits down at the table. I roll my eyes and slump into the kitchen where my cousins, Laiqa and Sana, stand waiting for me.

VII

Bleary with sleep,
your pupils glitter in the darkness.
I can feel them on my face
as I squint.

This night there are no shapes,
just a swathe of shadow;
I cannot understand why your eyes glitter,
and what they reflect.

Ghost Stories

In my cousin Sana's pitch-black bedroom, the clock blinks an angry, red 12:43 AM. I hear her soft breathing next to me as the rain and wind batter the window, muffled by thick drapes. I exhale. The sound of my aunt and uncle murmuring in their room has finally disappeared and the hallway outside of Sana's closed door is silent.

"I think we're good," I whisper into the air, not moving for fear the footboard I recline against will creak.

The bed dips next to me as Sana leans over in the darkness. A sudden, loud click pierces the air as she turns on her bedside lamp. I tut and squeeze my eyes shut against the invasion of buzzing, fluorescent light. I crack them open to reveal my cousin's sheepish grin. Wild, dark hair shrouds her face as she retracts her arm, then falls back against the headboard. We lean against opposite sides of the bed; we'd been chatting before we turned the lights off to fool my aunt and uncle. The blinds quiver behind the curtains as Sana opens her mouth to speak.

"Shh, I think I heard something," I say, stopping her. She freezes. We squint at the closed door across from the bed. Over the sound of the rain, we make out a muffled thud and the slow squeak of a hinge. Then, out in the hallway, we hear soft footsteps. I can't tell if they belong to my aunt. We shoot panicked glances at each other, then stare at the door breathless, fearing a parent's wrath. The brass doorknob turns slowly and Laiqa, Sana's sister, pokes her head into the room. I release my breath. Laiqa tiptoes into the room, followed by Asifa. Sana glares at her younger sisters, her eyes darkened by stark shadows.

"Why are you guys butting in here? You should be sleeping," Sana whispers. Laiqa and Asifa reply with twisting scowls.

"We wanna hang out with Mina. It's not fair that you get to hog her!" Asifa whines.

"Shut up! Do you want to wake the parents? Stop invading my room and go back to bed," Sana says, glancing at me. "We're gonna talk. Private stuff. Get lost."

"But you wanna talk to us, right Mina?" Asks Asifa. She and Laiqa give me their best beseeching eyes, drooping their mouths and sticking out their bottom lips in identical expressions.

I sigh in defeat. Sana rolls her eyes but doesn't argue. I sit up and fold my legs under me, making room for the two girls to sit on Sana's large, fluffy bed. After some shuffling around and a quick squabble over who will get the better spot against the headboard next to Sana, the girls settle down.

"So, what were you guys talking about?" Asifa asks. Sana and I trade secretive grins.

"Taxes," we say in unison. Laiqa groans.

"Alright fine, don't tell us," Laiqa says and then frowns, looking thoughtful. "By the way Mina, Auntie said something weird about you the other day and I wanted to know what you did for her to say that."

"Really?" I ask, leaning forward with interest. "Well, what did she say?"

"She said that you were...special. Like, you live in a different world." Sana barks out a laugh.

"Ha! You totally do Mina, you weirdo," she says, and winks at me. I stick my tongue out at her in retaliation.

"Huh," I grunt, turning my attention back to Laiqa. "What is that even supposed to mean?" I ask. Laiqa shrugs her shoulders and continues.

"Something about scaring her at night with your talk." The buzzing lamp overhead flickers. I pause for a moment trying to remember, scrunching my eyebrows together and squinting my eyes in thought.

"Ohhhh," I giggle. "I remember now. I freaked her out a bit the other day with some science talk."

"Science talk?" Asifa asks, "What's so scary about science?" Laiqa and Sana face me, equally confused.

I stare at my cousins, wondering where to begin. Outside, the wind and rain intensify, rattling the windowpane. A car alarm goes off. My knees begin to ache from the awkward way I'm sitting.

"Well, not science, I suppose, more like scientific theories. Alternate universes, for example." I flatten my palm on the bed underneath me and trail my fingers across the cold comforter.

"If you look at the world around us," I start looking around the room. "This bed is solid. We can touch it and feel it. We can see the things in this room because of the way the light interacts with the cones and rods in our eyes. We can smell things because of the receptors in our nose and feel things because of the nerves in our body."

I reach out and take Laiqa's hand, tickling her palm with the tips of my fingers. "You can only feel my hand, for example, because you have the hardware designed to feel it. If you didn't have nerves sending signals to your brain and translating that feeling to your consciousness, you wouldn't be able to feel anything. If you didn't have eyes, you wouldn't be able to see what's around you. All of our perceptions depend on our hardware: our bodies. Right?"

I look into each of their eyes and wait for their wide-eyed nods before continuing.

"So, we can only sense the dimension around us, the one that we are biologically designed to sense. But, there could be multiple dimensions coexisting in the same space, on the same plane, parallel to each other. We just might not have the hardware to be able to sense them, or anything that exists in them. Like if something was two-dimensional, it wouldn't be able to understand something three-dimensional. Get it?"

"I think so…" says Laiqa. Her voice trails off in confusion. Outside, the rain turns to a light patter. The sound of water trickling through a drain pipe seeps through the heavy curtain.

I release her hand and slowly raise both of mine

in front of me. I twirl my fingers through the still air and watch as miniscule specks of dust swirl around them, highlighted by the lamplight. Laiqa follows my movements, her eyes transfixed and glittering. I shrug, placing my hands back in my lap.

"Who's to say that there aren't beings existing right here and right now, just in a different, imperceptible dimension? Around us and through us, or whatever the equivalent of that is. And maybe we just can't sense their presence. And maybe they can't sense ours. Or maybe they can… or maybe we can too."

The girls still, eyes narrowing to digest my words. I can hear a distant plane cutting through the night sky. The standing lamp hums and flickers. For a beat, my cousins just stare at me and I stare coolly back. Laiqa doesn't say a word, her expression brooding. The shadows of her eyelashes stretch across her cheeks. I look down at my fingers as I twist and wring my hands.

Asifa blinks first.

"Yo, you're really creepy sometimes Mina," she says, with a nervous laugh.

"That's beside the point," I say. "We've all heard stories of angels and aliens and djinns—hidden beings that can appear and disappear at will. We know that our eyes are limited. We can't see everything that exists around us and it's not that crazy to think about how these creatures travel."

"But that stuff doesn't really exist, does it?" Laiqa asks. "They're just stories."

"Maybe. Stories have to come from somewhere too though. If a whole group of honest people swear that they saw an angel, it's really easy to dismiss it as superstition, but *something* happened. They didn't just make it up." Laiqa looks pensive and Asifa simply stares, wide-eyed, her mouth hanging open. As my thoughts race with possibilities, I whisper more forcefully, trying to explain them somehow.

"Don't certain religions believe that spirits can cross between worlds during certain times of the year? Where did that belief come from? And what if the thing we call a 'soul' actually exists in a different dimension, but is still somehow linked to the body until this physical body dies? I mean, we've all heard about how the spirits of the recently dece–"

BAM!

A loud knock from the other side of the wall interrupts me, and we all flinch. Asifa lets out a little scream. A muted, frustrated groan rises up to accompany the knock from the room next to us. I swivel towards the digital clock on the side table. It blinks 1:21 AM.

We fix our eyes on the wall as I lower my voice to a whisper. "Crap. I forgot Nabeela was sleeping in there."

"Yeah," Sana says. "I think she's got class in the morning." She turns to Laiqa and Asifa. "You guys should get to bed."

"Nooo," Asifa whines. "I wanted to hear about the dead people!" She looks at me and sulks. I chuckle.

"And I'm the creepy one?" I ask, raising one

eyebrow. Sana, eyes narrowed, glowers at Asifa.

"No, I'm tired, just go sleep!" She scolds. Asifa pouts in response but shuffles off the bed anyway. She battles Sana with her petulant stare, hand now on the doorknob. Sana wins of course. She's older. Asifa slinks out of the room, and we watch her sidestep the creaky sections of the floor to get to her own room. The door to my aunt and uncle's room is still wide open.

"Great, the idiot didn't even close the door behind her," Sana whispers. Then she turns to Laiqa. "You, why are you still here?" Laiqa glares back.

"What did I do? Asifa was the one being annoying! Can't I stay?" She huffs.

"No, you need to leave too. This is my room, and I'm telling you to get out!"

"Shhh," I interject. Sana and Laiqa quiet down but continue to glare at each other.

"What are you guys going to talk about anyways when I leave, huh?" Laiqa asks, peering at us through hooded, suspicious eyes.

"Shut up and go Laiqa! You think we're going to

talk right now? It's 2:00 AM. I want to sleep. Now get out!" Sana scolds with undue anger. Laiqa turns to me.

"See how she treats me Mina? She's always yelling at me for no reason."

"Laiqa," I say calmly. "I think you should sleep. There's no point in getting angry right now. Besides, I'm sleepy." Laiqa sighs, eyes downcast. She gets off the bed and walks to the door .

"Fine," she concedes. "I'm leaving." She turns around and looks at Sana. "You don't have to be so mean about it though."

"Don't freak out if the temperature in your room changes suddenly Laiqa!" I tease behind her. She turns to throw me a quick glare.

"Stop it!" she whines. Then, twisting the door handle, she walks out, shutting the door quietly behind her. I shuffle to the right side of the bed. Grabbing a pillow, I stretch out beside Sana. She reaches over, turns off the lamp, and plunges us into darkness once again. I hear her fluff her pillows and lie down as my eyes gradually adjust to the change. She turns towards me. I can see only the whites of her eyes. I snigger.

"You don't think they'll have nightmares like when they were kids do you?" I ask Sana.

"Who cares," she says. "Let's get back to the ghosts."

VIII

Like the frivolous décor taped to the wall,
you want to plaster
the wide, toothy grin,
from your own face onto mine.

But a smile is not made with the mouth.
And on this face with worried eyes,
you've pasted a grimace.

Grandiose Gestures

With a huff, I collapse into one of the many wooden chairs in the hall and put my feet up on the chair next to me, leaning to the side. For the last five hours, I've been decorating a little hall in a little church in the little German town of Völklingen for my cousin Amna's wedding. Our rental agreement for the hall is only for two days, so all of the decorating for the Mehndi (Henna Ceremony) tomorrow must be done last-minute.

Me, my sister Mahira, and three of our close cousins, Sana, Laiqa and Asifa, have flown from Canada to Germany where my aunt, Amna's mom, lives. They hadn't expected us to come since the marriage was arranged just a few months ago, but it wouldn't do for Amna to miss out on our company at her wedding. Not being there for our sister was unfathomable.

My sister and my cousins are in various positions around the hall. I am the only one in a nap position, and I expect I'll be called out for it soon. Baaria is up behind the bar, shuffling and reshuffling colourful, glass candy jars for optimal synergy. Amna, the bride-to-be, helps Sana tape up the strings of green and white balloons to make a canopy, and Mahira fiddles with the wires of the speaker system, trying in vain to bring it to life. When we arrived this morning, the gruff, old, caretaker of the hall told us the speakers had blown out after the last party and that we wouldn't be able to use them.

For a moment, I survey our handiwork. The colourful main display table, our glorious creation, is set up against the front wall of the small hall. It is the most important part of any Mehndi: the backdrop of every picture and the bride's seating area. The jewelled, South Asian drapes and light-adorned, jangly trimmings that usually accompany the main display at Mehndis were not available in Völklingen, so we had to persevere through collective thriftiness.

The napkin flowers we folded for hours in impromptu assembly lines are strung up in garlands, hanging in stark contrast to the deep pinks, rich greens, and vibrant yellows of the wrapping paper backdrop. The papers are solid blocks of colour instead of a more traditional mix of hanging, tie-dyed dupattas (scarves), giving the main display a modern feel. The glinting diyé (clay oil lamps) we've placed on the front table perfectly equidistant from each other are the result of four nights of sculpting and drying, and painting and drying, and giggling and whispering until dawn. Each one is hand-moulded and painted; they are slightly misshapen—a product of several sculptors—but beautiful nonetheless.

The table that holds them isn't a table at all, but a stepped display of stacked cardboard boxes, that's held together with generous amounts of packing tape and covered with a green silk bedsheet. Even the hundreds of balloons hanging above us are filled with our very breath, and I am out of it.

It's all for Amna, of course. She is the first of our group to get married; our first chance to be in that exclusive bridesmaid club; purveyors of the bride's wishes in every aspect of wedding planning. Tomorrow, on the day of the Mehndi, we will lead the folk songs, and sit in a tight, main circle on the floor around the dholki (two-sided hand drum) instead of on the fringes of the hoard of singing women.

Sana catches me staring at our display and we share a satisfied grin. As she places a small round Mehndi table near the feature wall, Waqas Bhai, the groom, saunters in carrying a couple dozen, flashy orange and yellow roses. I grimace at the cheesy, romantic gesture. Amna heads towards her fiancé to receive the flowers, but he greets her, side-steps her and goes instead towards our display. She stares after him. The rest of us throw around raised, questioning eyebrows and answering shrugs. Since none of us know the groom, we try to discern whether this behaviour is precedent-setting or not. He stops next to the front display and addresses us, energetic, like the host of a game show.

"Surprise everyone! You've been working really hard to decorate this place, so that's it girls," he says. "It's my turn to do something. I'm not going to tell you my plans. You'll just have to wait and see!"

We pause and shoot uneasy glances at each other as he edges closer to our beloved display wall and snatches up the tape.

He picks up a rose. He shoves a long stem diagonally onto the papered wall, right under a white napkin flower. Then he smashes tape onto it. My eyes widen with panic. I look to Amna, who watches Waqas Bhai with bemusement, but says nothing. Then, she shrugs her shoulders, and heads towards the back of the hall to arrange the seating area. The girls follow her lead and continue their own tasks. But I stay and watch.

Waqas Bhai begins by covering the yellow paper with roses. It wrinkles and sags under the weight, abused by the shiny clear tape. The white of the napkin flowers are overpowered by the onslaught of bright roses which clash with the deep colours of the wrapping paper. It's destruction. Waqas Bhai turns towards us with a glinting smile and excited eyes.

"What do you think?" He asks. The girls pause and look up at the roses.

I am unable to speak. The wild stems stick out every which way, mocking our five hours of work. I can barely breathe. I level a glare at him, hoping it's subtle enough to be considered accidental.

"It looks really bad," I murmur.

Concern colours Waqas Bhai's features. Baaria and Mahira look at me scandalised, standing close enough to hear my blunt words. They come over to me and start whispering furiously:

"You can't just say that Mina! He's going to think we're so rude!" Says Baaria.

"Oh my God, keep your opinion to yourself,"

Mahira scolds, "You can say you personally don't like it, but don't just go saying it's bad! He's only trying to do something nice for Amna."

Despite their protests, my eyes do not waver, holding Waqas Bhai's gaze. His expression slowly morphs into a lopsided grin.

"That's okay," he says, raising a commanding finger. "I will change your mind. Just you wait until I finish. You're going to love it, I'm sure." Then, he turns around and starts taping roses onto the green paper. I don't reply, and instead whisper to the girls.

"Come on guys, admit it. It looks terrible. We worked so hard on everything. It looked perfect, and he just swoops in with some flowers? He's turning our modern Mehndi into a FOB fail!" They grimace. Baaria is wide-eyed and worried as I express my ire. The muscles in her long neck strain as she tries to placate me and avoid a scene.

"He's just trying to be nice Mina," she says. "Maybe he wants to show that he's invested in this marriage? And Amna doesn't really mind, I'm sure."

Laiqa walks in through the main door of the hall and catches the tail end of our conversation before interrupting.

"Uhhh guys?" She lifts an eyebrow and points her thumb back towards the door. "I was just outside, and Waqas Bhai's entire trunk is full of roses."

"What?" I hiss in disbelief and jump out of my chair, imagining how the paper would be torn off the wall under the weight of so many garish flowers. Laiqa purses her lips, contorting them to one side of her face, and offers a resigned shrug.

"Yeah, I'm not exaggerating. The entire trunk."

"Is he crazy?" I exclaim. "Where did he even get them in this town? Amna!" I cry out, begging for some support. Amna jogs over from across the room, alarmed. "Please Amna," I plead. "You have to stop him!" Amna scrunches up her face and gives her head a meek shake, shuffling her feet.

"I don't really want to create an issue with him. We're only just getting to know each other, you know. It's okay. I don't really mind. There has to be some give and take."

I'm incredulous. What about our hard work, our vision? Is undue patience a matrimonial by-product?

I flop down, defeated. Sana joins me. She's been quiet, but I watch her hands for a moment as she twists them anxiously. We watch Waqas Bhai finish his work with masochistic fascination. He covers the entire wall and a couple of chairs with his gaudy roses.

"Is this how it's going to be for her?" I ask Sana. "Just letting him do whatever he wants, just to avoid an argument? His style is so different from hers." Sana crosses her long arms and looks down towards her lap.

"I dunno, man. I couldn't do it. Marrying someone from Pakistan with such cheesy, outdated tastes? How outdated must his beliefs be? I don't know how she tolerates it. Just goes with the flow maybe?"

"Yeah, I guess," I sigh. Amna comes by to check up on us, and I plead again. "Please Amna, could you ask him to at least cut the stems off or something? The wallpaper will definitely fall. It's already so wrinkled." Amna sighs. Her large round eyes are hesitant, but she gives in.

"Alright, let me talk to him." She trudges over to Waqas Bhai and softly calls him. He turns towards her with a blinding smile, excited to hear her words. She mumbles something to him and points at the walls. His eyes, still intently on her, widen in understanding, and then he gives a vigorous nod of his head and fetches a pair of scissors. He trims half the stem off each flower.

Sana sits beside me, reduced to tears at the sight of the drooping, crumpled, and oversaturated feature wall.

"I am never decorating again," she mutters bitterly. "Or getting married."

Carrying another pile of roses, Waqas Bhai shoots us a smile as he saunters by.

About the Author

Manahil Pasha lives in Mississauga with her family. She's a fresh graduate, holding a bachelor's degree in English, French, and Professional Writing & Communication from the University of Toronto.

One of her aspirations is to help people around the world be more connected through empathy and understanding. She therefore explores human relationships and the intricacies of their communication in her writing. *Faces* is her first book, and she hopes, a pathway to many more.

Acknowledgements

My sincere gratitude to Professor Guy Allen, for his guidance and encouragement throughout the process of making this book. Thank you to Nick West, my copyeditor, for bringing a unique perspective to my stories and helping them blossom. Thank you to my sister, Maryam Pasha, who transformed my messy doodles into the beautiful cover of this book.

I'd also like to thank Laurel Waterman, who not only taught me the rules of good writing, but also what it is to be a good writer. And a final thanks to my fellow classmates in WRI420. I learned a lot from each of you.

www.ingramcontent.com/pod-product-compliance
Lightning Source LLC
Chambersburg PA
CBHW061334040426
42444CB00011B/2921